Old AYR

by

R & J KENNEDY

Crossing the river at Doonfoot in 1923

© 1992 R & J Kennedy
First Published in the United Kingdom, 1992
Reprinted 1994
By Richard Stenlake, Ochiltree Sawmill, The Lade,
Ochiltree, Ayrshire KA18 2NX
Tel: 02907 266

ISBN 1-872074-19-7

The Sandgate, Ayr

Sandgate House can be seen, front right, in this 1920 view of the Sandgate. The site is now occupied by Ayr's main Post Office, built in 1968.

INTRODUCTION

Ayr's recorded history is usually considered to date from 1197 when William the Lion ordered a wooden castle to be built between the mouths of the Rivers Ayr and Doon. It is thought that the present Ayr Academy occupies the site of the old castle. In 1205 the settlement beside the castle was granted a Royal Charter and so the Royal Burgh of Ayr came into being.

Ayr's growth both as a market town and as a focus for foreign trade is easy to understand. It was protected by a Royal Castle, was situated at a convenient crossing point on the River Ayr and was able to build a safe harbour at the river mouth. In fact, in the 16th Century it was the leading seaport in the West of Scotland. The building of the imposing Church of St. John the Baptist in the 13th Century also bears witness to the importance attached to the town.

The town was threatened by Vikings in 1263, suffered an English occupation in 1296 which culminated in the burning of the enemy troops in the 'Barns of Ayr' by William Wallace in 1297 and had its castle destroyed by Robert the Bruce in 1298 to prevent it falling into the hands of the auld enemy. On a more peaceful note, in 1315 Robert the First held a Parliament in the Church of St. John in order to settle the succession to the Scottish throne.

The 15th Century was mostly a period of consolidation for the town. Many of the wooden houses were replaced by more substantial dwellings, a Tolbooth was built in the High Street and the old wooden bridge across the river was replaced by a stone one - the Auld Brig of Ayr.

The next century saw a dramatic upturn in the town's prosperity. The High Street was extended to the Townhead but even then was hard pressed to accommodate the fish, meal, sheep, wool, cattle and horse markets held there each week. In spite of the blowing sand, the Sandgate was further developed, the Malt Cross was erected at its junction with the High Street and the town's second Tolbooth built at its widest part. The harbour was greatly improved and, in spite of the considerable expenditure involved, the town remained virtually debt free. By 1600 the population had grown to about 2000 living in 400 houses.

The appearance of the area south of the harbour was greatly changed in 1652 when Cromwell, during his military occupation of Scotland, built a huge fort or Citadel, some of whose walls can still be seen today. The fort incorporated the Church of St. John and to compensate for this loss, Cromwell made a gift of one third of the cost towards the building of a replacement church - the Auld Kirk of Ayr.

Ayr's affluence declined during the next 100 years, with little change in size or population. This slide was halted in the late 18th Century when improved communications by mail and stage coaches made Ayr an important link between Glasgow and South West Scotland. A further 100 years on, helped by the arrival of the railway in 1840, Ayr was expanding rapidly. Many elegant houses were built and a large number of commercial and industrial businesses were established, all now within easy reach of Glasgow by rail.

The town then continued to move towards, then into the 20th Century. Newton on Ayr was incorporated in 1873. Beach facilities were improved to cater for the fast growing holiday trade and a new station complex was opened in 1886. The Council in 1898 set up its own Electric Generating Company and followed this in 1901 by opening a Tramway System.

With the advent of the picture postcard at the beginning of the 20th Century, photographic records of changes and developments in towns such as Ayr became readily available. Many such postcards have been used in this book to illustrate the changing face of the town since 1900.

R. & J. Kennedy, October 1992.

Many and varied industrial and commercial establishments were crammed into the Wallacetown district of Ayr at the turn of the century. Easily identified in this picture are the American Steam Laundry, D. Brown (Cash Drapers at the junction of Wallace Street and George Street), Speirs Iron Plane Works, A. Ballantyne (Joiner & Glazier), the Carrick Brass works and C. Buchanan (Watchmaker). Virtually the whole area has been recently redeveloped, but the frontage of the Roman Catholic Chapel, top right, is still recognisable.

Ayr, Station Hotel.

The east end of Burns Statue Square presents an air of peace and tranquility which well reflects the pace of life 80 years ago. The Station Hotel, opened in 1886 together with the new passenger rail terminus, advertised in 1910 a weekend break with first class rail travel from St. Enochs Station and hotel accommodation for 25/-. The statue of a soldier is a memorial to the men of the Royal Scots Fusiliers who died in campaigns fought between 1877 and 1902. The terrible conditions they encountered are shown by the fact that most died as a result of disease rather than by enemy action.

The Ayr Entertainment and Roller Skating Rink with its impressive frontage was situated in Boswell Park and provided for the popular pastime of roller skating in the early 1900s. However, with the coming of the 'movies' it closed its doors early in October 1910 only to re-open at the end of the same month as the Ayr Electric Pavilion showing films. It was later renamed Greens Playhouse.

Main Street, Ayr.

Travelling to Prestwick from Ayr along Main Street would appear to have been a much less daunting prospect in 1913 than it is today with only a bicycle, a horse and cart and an Ayr bound tram to contend with. An outstanding survivor of recent road redevelopment is Newton Steeple which is now isolated on an island in the middle of the King Street-Main Street junction. Constructed in 1795 as the entrance to the old Newton-on-Ayr Parish Church, it is the only part of the church to survive. The site of the two low buildings opposite the Steeple was used in 1932 to build the Orient Cinema, so called because of its oriental type turret and interior decorations. The building remains in use today as a bingo hall.

September 1902 saw the opening of the New Gaiety Theatre in Carrick Street. It was purpose-built to present drama, musicals, variety and film shows and replaced the Caledonian Theatre which had stood on the same site. In 1925 the theatre was taken over by the Popplewell family and from then on the cast lists read like a Who's Who of variety - Harry Lauder, Will Fyffe, Sid Fields, Robert Wilson, Chick Murray, Jack Milroy, Rikki Fulton etc. The Gaiety has survived two serious threats to its future. In 1955 it had to be rebuilt after a fire and in 1972 a redevelopment plan was thwarted by the theatre becoming a listed building. In 1973 it was taken over by Ayr Town Council and today it still stands as one of the last out-posts of live entertainment in Scotland.

John Colquhoun operated his business from premises off Prestwick Road. These consisted of a single room for himself and an outhouse for his mule. While he would at times undertake odd jobs for local firms, his main occupation was as a rag and bone man. He would barter home-made flags, banners, windmills and his famous candy for rags, bones and old iron with the local children.

RECRUITING STAFF BARRACKS AYR 1917

On the 1st April 1873 the Royal North British Fusiliers became Ayrshire's County Regiment as a result of the localisation scheme, Ayr Barracks being the depot for the regiment. In 1881 the name of the regiment was changed to the Royal Scots Fusiliers and two years later the bullet-riddled colours of the 1st Battalion were handed over to the custody of the Auld Kirk of Ayr where they can still be seen. The Barracks were renamed Churchill Barracks in 1942 and after they were vacated by the Regiment, now called the Royal Highland Fusiliers as a result of amalgamation, the Council acquired the site using it to provide a location for Codona's shows and in 1972 to build the new swimming baths. This picture shows the 1918 RSF recruiting staff posed on the shooting range at the Barracks.

The bottom of the High Street is seen in an unusually deserted mood in this 1938 photograph, taken shortly before the two corner properties containing the empty shops were demolished. The original plan to use this space for road widening was soon abandoned when it was realised that this would entail removing some of the historic buildings in New Bridge Street, and a small garden, still to be seen today, was laid out. A branch of Woolworth's Stores, the first of the large multiples to open in Ayr, occupies the site of the King's Arms Hotel which was demolished in 1925. This had been one of Ayr's finest 19th Century Inns and was, at that time, the departure point for both passenger and mail coaches to Kilmarnock and Glasgow.

Many of the happy holidaymakers relaxing round the Steven Fountain on Ayr seafront in 1905 would not realise that they were being looked down upon by the inmates of Ayr Prison (the building in the background). It was known as "The Cottage by the Sea" to many of the prisoners. Although the fountain is still in working order today most of the jail building was demolished and replaced by the western end of the County Buildings, constructed in 1931. With the closing of the jail, local residents lost the carpet cleaning services that had been provided by the prisoners.

The Ayr Fertiliser Works owned by Daniel Wyllie & Co. were situated on Newton sea front and are typical of the many industries that flourished in Ayr in the first half of the century. A few well-remembered examples are Grays Carpet Factory, Lees Boot & Shoe St. Crispin Works, Templetons Woollen Mills, Beebee's Tannery and Turners Breweries. The changing face of the town is well illustrated by the fact that none of the firms exist today although the fertiliser works buildings are still used by a number of companies. The part of the esplanade in front of the works is much used by local sea anglers.

Virginia Gardens, Ayr.

The appearance of this quiet street of late Victorian red sandstone houses has changed little in the 70 years since this photograph was taken. Its peacefulness belies the fact that it is only a few yards from the very busy Ayr-Prestwick Road, just south of Tam's Brig.

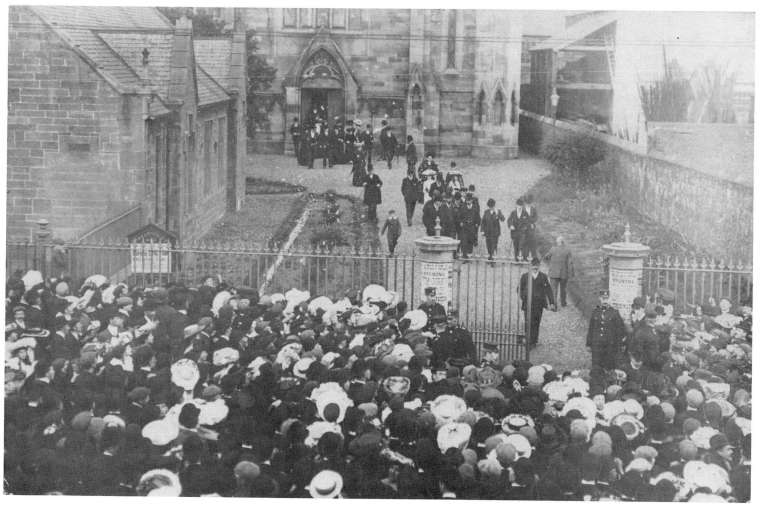

A near riot took place in Main Street, Ayr on Sunday 2nd July 1905. The congregation of Newton United Free Church had been evicted and the incoming Free Church congregation held their first service on that day. A crowd of about 4000 protesters gathered, eggs were thrown, worshippers were jostled and the crowd had to be controlled by the whole Ayr police force with batons drawn. Posters concerning the eviction can be seen at the gate of the church.

The South Quay and slipway at Ayr Harbour were crowded on the 11th June 1910 when the Countess of Glasgow launched the new Ayr lifeboat, the Janet Hoyle, presented to the town by the RNLI. It replaced the previous Janet Hoyle which had been endowed by Thomas Hardie of London and named after his wife. Ayr's first lifeboat was donated to the Harbour Trust in 1803 to help safeguard the ships visiting the busy harbour. The wooden erection on the right of the photograph was used by many generations of Ayr youths as a convenient, if rather dangerous, diving platform.

The earliest recorded horse race to be run over the Old Racecourse at Seafield took place in October 1775 for a purse of £50 and racing continued there until 1906. The site, abandoned by the Western Meeting in 1907, has since been put to good use. Part of it forms some of the holes of Ayr Seafield golf course and the remainder is laid out in sports pitches for local schools and clubs. Part of the old stand was retained and used as changing room accommodation.

James Gilchrist Ltd, Land O'Burns Bakeries, in Boswell Park was one of the town's best known bakers' shops. The tearoom situated above the shop was a popular meeting place for morning coffee and 'star spotting' was often possible as the cast of the nearby Gaiety Theatre frequented it during rehearsal breaks. The site was later developed as a Tesco Supermarket which closed recently and has been replaced by a large car park.

AYR UNITED FOOTBALL CLUB—Season 1921-22.

Players—Left to Right—Back Row—Quaite (Trainer), Cunningham, Quinn, Smith, Nisbet, McCloy, Slade.
Front Row—McDougall, Hogg, McBain (Captain), Gibson, Low.

Ayr United Football and Athletic Club was formed in April 1910 by the amalgamation of Ayr F.C. and Ayr Parkhouse. Their first match was played at Somerset Park, home of Ayr F.C. from 1888, in August 1910 and resulted in a 2-0 victory over Port Glasgow Athletic. This 1921-22 team must represent the heyday of the club. Neil McBain played several times for Scottish International sides and Jock Smith and Phil McCloy were Scotland's full-back pairing in the 1924 team which drew 1-1 with England in the first international to be played at Wembley.

19

George Street, Ayr.

One of the best known characters in Ayr in the earlier half of this century was Johnny Ramsay whose grocer's shop in the Wallacetown district of Ayr is seen in this photograph. As well as being a prominent business man, he was a leading member of the Magic Circle and entertained his customers with his sleight of hand when dispensing their orders. Joining George Street at this point were Wallace Street from the left and John Street from the right.

The Proclamation of Accession of George V on 10th May 1910 was first read in Ayr on the steps of the County Buildings by the Sheriff Clerk and the reading was repeated at the site of the Old Malt Cross and Burns Statue Square. The Guard of Honour in the procession, seen here in Wellington Square, was mounted by men of the RSF resplendent in their scarlet tunics. Thousands thronged the route to view the colourful spectacle.

One of Ayr's most attractive beauty spots, the River Ayr Walk, on the south bank of the river was opened in 1910 by Mrs Oswald of Auchincruive. On the river edge just below an old deserted limekiln, a fresh water spring rises from a hollow in the rock. Tradition has it that the indentation was caused by William Wallace's heel as he jumped across the river to escape pursuing English soldiers. Unfortunately the ladle, at one time fastened to the rock beside the spring, has long since gone.

Tam's Brig, Ayr.

Tam's Brig was constructed in the 1850s when Ayr's passenger station was transferred from the North Harbour to Townhead and a bridge was needed to carry the Ayr-Prestwick Road over the new line. The bridge was probably named after Tom McCreath the farmer of Bellesleyhill Farm, who is said to have persuaded the builders to allow him to be first to cross the bridge when it was opened. The street trader is selling his wares at the end of Elmbank Street.

The first review of Territorial Forces in Ayr took place on the Low Green on 8th June 1912. Before a crowd of over ten thousand spectators, Lord Eglinton, the Lord Lieutenant of the County, inspected (among others) detachments of Artillery, Yeomanry, National Reserves and Crimean Veterans. The photograph shows the representatives from the Ambulance Service and the Red Cross.

The photographer who took this 1905 picture of Ayr High Street featured, on the left, two of the town's best known drinking establishments, the Sun Inn Bar and Matha Dickie's Ayr Arms Hotel. At this time the street boasted 20 hotels and inns which could account for the Loan Office seen on the other side of the street. The Sun Inn also acted as a departure point for local carriers with regular services to Dalrymple, Kirkmichael, Kirkoswald, Ochiltree and Straiton. With the closure in 1985 of the Ayr Arms, now part of the Kyle Centre, the High Street became publess.

Ayr Academy former pupils played their full part in the first World War and the War Memorial in the main hall of the school lists the names of four staff and one hundred and eleven former pupils who lost their lives during the hostilities. The pupils involved themselves in war savings schemes supporting war charities and raising money to finance Ayr Academy War Beds in overseas field hospitals. Sales of postcards was one of these money raising ventures.

New Bridge, Ayr

In the late 18th Century the volume of traffic across the River Ayr was such that the Auld Brig could not cope and a New Bridge based on a Robert Adam design was built. It survived for less than 100 years, suffering such severe damage in 1877 that it had to be rebuilt. The buildings at the end of the present New Bridge are little changed from this 1925 view and provide an attractive entry to the town from the North.

Sadly this view of Beresford Terrace and Killoch Place no longer exists today. The attractive houses on the left have been demolished and replaced by a modern bank building and an island and traffic lights have been erected at the junction with Miller road. The white pillars mark the entrance to No.1 Burns Statue Square which in this 1923 photograph is a Palais de Danse. Later it became well known as the Bobby Jones Ballroom. Built as the RSF Drill hall in 1901, it housed the Scottish Electric Picture Palace for a time from 1909. In recent years it has been used as a Bingo Hall and an amusement arcade.

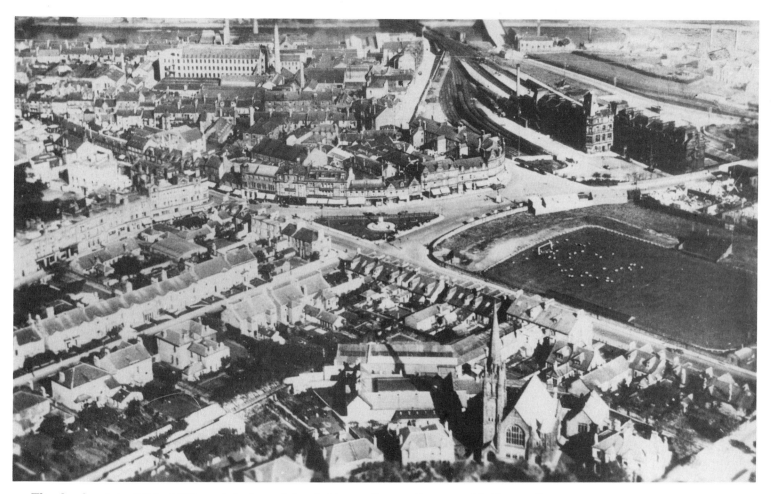

The focal point of this 1928 aerial view of Ayr is Burns Statue Square with Burns Statue and the surrounding gardens. On the right sheep are seen grazing on Beresford Park football pitch, now the site of the Odeon Cinema and Safeway supermarket. Above is the imposing building of Ayr Station Hotel. The large factory, top left, is Templeton's Woollen Mills in Mill Street. This was not the most pleasant street to walk along on a hot day as it also contained Beebee's Tannery and the local slaughter house. None of these businesses exist there today.

CHARLIE KEMBLE'S SUPER ENTERTAINERS.

AYR PAVILION.   SEASON 1928.

Willie Larmer	Dave Bruce	Tommy Dale	John Hilton	Jack Anthony	
Jennie Collings	Nana Mason	Charlie Kemble	Maie Wynne	Peggy Mason	PHOTO GEDDES.

The entrance to Ayr Pavilion acts as a background for this 1928 photograph of Charlie Kemble Entertainers. They appeared there each summer from 1926 till 1929 and so popular was the show that after the first week in 1926 they had to change from once nightly to twice nightly performances. Charlie Kemble returned in 1932 with the 'Merrymakers' and excerpts from the show were broadcast on BBC Radio. On the right is a young Jack Anthony starting on the road to stardom. The performers trod the same stage where immortals such as Florrie Ford and Will Fyffe had appeared in the previous decade.

Although the Pavilion or 'Piv' as it is known only dates back to 1911, the balusters at the front of the building originally formed part of Ayr's first New Bridge. This unusual four turreted building, standing at the north end of the Low Green had been put to wide-ranging uses during its lifetime. Leased to the Popplewell family in 1913, the local nickname of 'The White Elephant by the Sea' was difficult to overcome but they succeeded by presenting top class variety, which drew large crowds. It has also housed dancing, roller skating, film shows, boxing and opera. Recently doubts have arisen about its future but it still offers discos and live bands four nights a week.

Newmarket Street and Junior Conservative Club, Ayr.

Newmarket Street, so named when it was developed to link Sandgate to the new Buttermarket which was finally opened in 1814, has resisted change better than most of the older parts of Ayr. Although the street is now pedestrianised, the buildings seen here in 1905 are easily recognised today. The firm of Hugh Henry has only ceased trading in the last few years. The well dressed gentlemen are congregated outside the door of the Junior Conservative Club. Three heads above the door of the Macneille building on the other side of the street are thought to be of William Wallace, John Knox and Robert the Bruce.

When the foundations of the Auld Brig of Ayr were found to be unsafe in 1905, a controversy arose as to whether the Bridge should be repaired or pulled down. Finally repair work was commenced in 1907 and a temporary wooden bridge constructed. The scene shown above is the re-opening procession crossing the Bridge on July 19th 1910 led by Lord Rosebery, President of the Burns Federation, R.A. Oswald of Auchincruive and Provost Hunter. The Burgh Band is playing on the wooden bridge, which has been retained to act as a band stand. In the background the sign for a posting establishment is that of the Black Bull.

Alex Livesey, a native of Wales, was resident in Ayr for forty five years up to his death in 1931. Though well known as a book seller, trading from his two wheeled barrow in Ayr High Street, he was better known as a long distance walker. Starting with a Land's End to John O'Groats walk in 1882, his last walk of note took place in 1924. Wishing to visit the Wembley Exhibition he followed a route from Ayr to London to John O'Groats thence back to Ayr. He kept a record of his journey in a notebook which is full of comments written by shopkeepers, policemen and others he met on his way. J. Cunningham, a newsagent in Brora wrote on Aug 30th 1924 "Mr Livesey passed here at 7.45 p.m. in good spirits."

The memorial drinking fountain in the foreground of this 1936 view of Sandgate from Wellington Square was erected in 1868 in memory of Primrose William Kennedy, Provost of Ayr from 1853 to 1861 and a prominent banker in the town. When this photograph was taken the bus station, operated by the Western SMT Co. had both its entrance and exit opening directly onto the Sandgate.

Loudoun Hall standing in the Boat Vennel is the oldest house in Ayr. It was designed and built about 1500 for Thomas Tait a local merchant to provide a comfortable town-house dwelling. It is one of the earliest surviving examples of this type of house in Scotland. Through the years it deteriorated from being the home of the Sheriffs of Ayr to become a slum tenement. Rescued in the years following World War II, it has been gradually restored and is now used as a meeting place by a number of local societies and as a gallery by local artists. The left wing of the hall, seen here behind the lamp post, was demolished during the restoration.

"JUNO" AND "GLEN SANNOX" IN AYR HARBOUR

A holiday in Ayr without a trip on a pleasure steamer would have been almost unthinkable to holidaymakers in the first half of the Century. The 'Juno', berthed here at Ayr's South Quay alongside the 'Glen Sannox', was probably one of the best known of these pleasure craft, sailing from Ayr each summer from 1898 to 1932 with only a short break for war service. She was replaced by the 'Duchess of Hamilton'. Then in 1974 when it appeared that the tradition had died out, the Paddle Steamer Preservation Society started the popular cruises on the 'Waverley'.

Ayr, as a holiday resort, started off with the natural advantages of a sandy beach and safe bathing. The Town Council realised that further facilities would be needed to attract their share of the Clyde Coast holiday trade, growing rapidly at the turn of the century due to easier travel. Part of the esplanade had been built in 1881 and was later extended towards the Doon. Toilets and bathing machines were provided and the Council approved the introduction of donkey rides, boating and ice cream sales. The throng of well dressed holidaymakers in this 1910 view proves that their plans were successful.

One of Ayr's open-topped trams seen in 1913 outside the Olympia Bar which was situated at the junction of George Street and King Street, an area radically changed due to extensive redevelopment. The tram is en route from the racecourse via George Street and River Street to rejoin the main line at the New Bridge. The tramway system was opened in 1901 but with the move of Ayr Racecourse to the Craigie district in 1907 and increasing support at Somerset Park to watch the recently formed Ayr United, the tramway board saw the need for a branch line to cater for the sporting public and the Hawkhill or Racecourse branch was opened in August 1913.

Stepping Stones, River Ayr Walk, Ayr

Young ladies of 1910 posing on the stepping stones which, together with an attractive picnic area, were situated at the eastern end of the River Ayr Walk. A new generation of stones have taken their place, but the Overmills (seen in the background), have almost disappeared. With a history of corn milling dating back to the 14th Century when they were owned by the monks, the Overmills survived until 1963 when they were finally demolished.

Railway Station, Alloway

When the Glasgow & South Western Railway Company opened the Dunure & Maidens Light Railway in 1906 to cater mainly for golfers visiting the newly opened Turnberry Hotel, a station was built at Alloway. Near the station the line ran through a tunnel which had to be very carefully constructed as it was only a short distance from Alloway Auld Kirk. Passenger traffic on the line ceased in 1930 only to be reinstated in 1947 to take passengers as far as Butlins Holiday Camp at the Heads of Ayr. Final closure took place in 1968. Very few traces of the station remain today but the entrance to the tunnel is visible from the road into the Land O'Burns Centre.

ST. JOHN'S TOWER, AYR. 16

John Miller, a gunsmith to trade, having made his fortune in India returned to settle in Ayr. He purchased in 1853 the lands of the Barony of Montgomerieston on which stood the Tower of the Church of St. John. A house was built, attached to the Tower, where he lived until his death in 1910. A good amateur builder, 'Baron Miller' built the look-out tower on the wall of the fort in South Quay, now South Harbour Street. The turret is often known as Miller's Folly.

HIGH STREET, AYR.

89226 ⓦ

Traffic congestion in the Wallace Tower area is not only a problem of modern times. When this photograph was taken 70 years ago a mixture of motor cars, horse and hand carts and straying pedestrians must have made driving a hazardous affair. On the right is The Picture House whose foyer contained a very elegant tea room. The cinema was later renamed the Gaumont and today in its place stands a Littlewood's Store. The centre pole supports for the tram power lines were replaced in 1924 by wall brackets and one of these remains today on the wall of 140 High Street.

A busy Sandgate in the early thirties, the view being dominated by the imposing 225ft Town Steeple which together with the Town House below were completed in 1830 to a design drawn up by Thomas Hamilton. Beyond Terry's tobacconist shop on the right is seen the red sandstone front of Ayr's main Post Office which is now the Registrar's Office. Next door the building of the Ayr County Club has been incorporated in the Queens Court Shopping Centre.

BURNS STATUE SQUARE, ODEON PICTURE HOUSE, & ICE RINK, AYR   A.8837

When the Odeon Cinema in Burns Statue Square was opened in 1938 it became Ayr's sixth cinema, helping to cater for the voracious appetite for entertainment of the cinema-goers of that era. In those days there were thirteen programmes available each week in Ayr. It is now the only remaining cinema and offers a four screen facility. Green's Playhouse and the Orient have been converted to bingo halls, the Gaumont to a Littlewood's Store, the Ritz in New Road to a snooker club and the Regal in Prestwick Road is now Rosefield Motors.

In order to develop a new racecourse, the Western Meeting acquired the Blackhouse Estate north of the River Ayr in 1907. After extensive building of stands and enclosures, they established Ayr as the premier racecourse in Scotland and one of the finest in Britain. The September Race Week was a high spot in the social calendar, from the fine house parties of the local gentry to the funfare and sideshows set up in the centre of the track for the local punters, who were allowed free entry to that part of the course.

The Ayrshire Agricultural Association's Annual Show was first held in 1852 and soon it established a position as one of Scotland's most prestigious farming occasions. For 50 years from 1897 it was held in the Dam Park, moving in 1946 to its present venue at Ayr Racecourse. In order to appeal to the non-farming visitor, the Show included events such as the very popular dog show. The gentleman holding the Great Dane at a Dam Park Show in the twenties is Waistel Cooper of the well-known local firm of newspaper and fancy goods wholesalers.

Burns' Statue, Ayr   743

The most striking feature in this 1925 view of part of Burns Statue Square unfortunately can no longer be seen. The ornate wrought ironwork which surrounded the gardens was removed during WWII as a contribution to the war effort. Burns Statue, with the Bard looking south towards his birthplace in Alloway, was unveiled in 1891 and Burns lovers still congregate there each year on the anniversary of his birth. The attractive sandstone buildings at the top of Dalblair Road and in Burns Statue Square were designed by local architect James A. Morris.

A 594 Monument Road, Ayr

The foundation stone of the Burns Monument, situated in gardens on the banks of the Doon at Alloway, was laid in 1820 by Alexander Boswell of Auchinleck. The Monument seen here in the background was finally opened in 1823 after three and a half years of rather leisurely building. The record of subscriptions to the building fund contains some very interesting facts. Fifty guineas was given by the Prince Regent, later George IV, almost one third of the total of over £2000 came from overseas and the list of 700 subscribers contained only one woman, Lady Hamilton Cathcart. 50,000 visitors from all over the world visited the Monument in 1991.

The Milrig Hotel, in Charlotte Street, was a typical example of the many large houses in Ayr that were adapted to cater for summer visitors. In a 1930 brochure it was advertised as "A first class renowned establishment, excellent cuisine, with tennis court, putting green, summer houses, swings etc." The steps leading to the front door were built over the pavement and proved an irresistible challenge to many children walking to the beach. The building was demolished and the area is now a municipal car park.

The end of the line for the Ayr Tramway System with the dismantling of some of the cars at the Bellesleyhill Road Depot in 1932. The story began in 1883 when an Ayr and District Tramway Company was formed and the following year received Parliamentary approval to construct a horse drawn tramway in Ayr and Prestwick. This plan was dropped in 1888. After the opening of its own generating station in Mill Street, Ayr Town Council saw the opportunity to operate an electric system and Ayr Corporation trams started to run in 1901. The route initially was from Prestwick Cross to St. Leonard's Church via the High Street, a distance of four miles. Extensions to Burns Monument in 1902 and to the Racecourse in 1913 were later additions. The early twenties saw the tram business flourish and even in the second half of the decade, despite rising electricity costs and the competition of the railway and the private car, things seemed to be running smoothly. However, by 1931 the proposed cost of repairing ageing track and cars proved to be too high and the tramway was closed with the last car running on December 31st, 1931.

Main Street and Newton Cross, Ayr

Looking north in 1925 along Main Street from the New Bridge. In the right foreground is Newton Cross which was formerly sited in the middle of Main Street at the Newton Steeple. Beside the Campbeltown Bar, still in business today, is the impressive building of the Carnegie Library. In 1890 the local Library Committee invited Andrew Carnegie to give a lecture in the town. Unable to attend, he offered a grant for a new library of £10,000 on condition that the town adopted the Free Libraries Act. This being agreed, building began and the library was opened on 2nd September 1893.

A long tradition of entertaining both local inhabitants and holidaymakers with 'all the fun of the fair' has been established by the Codona family. Their funfair has visited Ayr for many years, particularly during the September Race
Week. Various venues have been used, such as Northfield and the Dam Park and here we see them set up on Ayr
Esplanade in 1935. At the time of writing in 1992 they were appearing on a space behind Ayr's swimming baths, not
a stone's throw from the location shown. The building in the background is part of Ayr Shipyard.

The Fort and Tennis Courts. Ayr

Overlooking the Fort tennis courts in Montgomerie Terrace stands the imposing Tower of St. John, the oldest building in Ayr. Part of the large Church of St. John the Baptist, the Tower has had a varied past. In 1315 it witnessed a Scottish Parliament held by Robert the Bruce in the Church, in 1654 it became part of Cromwell's Citadel together with the Church and surrounding lands and it survived the eventual destruction of the Church in 1726. Purchased by the Marquis of Bute in 1914, it was restored to its former state by the removal of 'Baron Miller's' additions. Since the tennis courts were recently resurfaced by the local council it would be difficult to find them as quiet as they are in this 1927 view.

AYR ICE RINK

A.8836

Ayr Ice Rink was opened in 1939 in Beresford Terrace and its large ice pad provided an ideal venue for skating, curling and ice hockey. For many years it was the only indoor curling surface in SW Scotland and rinks from as far afield as Stranraer and Dumfries were regular visitors. Ayr Raiders ice hockey team played to packed audiences in the early 1950s and the names of Domenico, Martini and Girard will bring back memories to most Scottish fans. The rink also hosted other sporting events such as basketball and professional tennis. It closed in 1972 and in its place there is now a Safeway Supermarket. A smaller rink was opened in Limekiln Road in 1973.

In the early 1920s the Paris Observatory, using the Eiffel Tower, transmitted a series of radio signals at fixed times each day to act as time checks. Wallace Allan, an enterprising Ayr Jeweller and Watchmaker, built a model of the Tower to which was attached a ball, arranged to fall coincidentally with one of these signals. An October morning in 1921 sees the crowd assembling around the window of his shop in Newmarket Street for the 10.45 a.m. time check.

The picture on the inside back cover is a late 19th century view of Hope Street, often known as 'Back of the Isle'. Wallace Allan took over the wine shop premises and has traded there for about 100 years.